SPACE FLYERS

Paper Airplane Book

63 Mini Planes to Fold and Fly

Ken Blackburn and **Jeff Lammers**

Workman Publishing, New York

To my mother—my role model for scientific curiosity, dedication, unconditional love; an amazing cook and best friend. —KB

To the spirit of aviation—paper airplanes are where everyone starts. —JL

Copyright © 2017 by Ken Blackburn and Jeff Lammers

Library of Congress Cataloging-in-Publication Data is available.

ISBN 978-0-7611-9379-1

Cover design by Vaughn Andrews
Interior design by Jean-Marc Troadec
Cover and interior photos by Walter Chrynwski
Plane graphics: Star Quest and Galaxy 800 by Shi Chen; Aerobot by Peter Hoey; Ardor by Brad Hamann; Alien Clipper by Jose Cruz; RKO by Chris Spollen; Spectre by Maurice Kessler; Gemini and Space Station by Mark Reidy; Mini World Record by Daniel Pelavin; Dynamo by Garth Glazier; Cosmojet by Robert Zimmerman.

Workman books are available at special discounts when purchased in bulk for premiums and sales promotions as well as for fund-raising or educational use. Special editions or book excerpts can also be created to specification. For details, please contact specialmarkets@hbgusa.com.

Workman Publishing Co., Inc., a subsidiary of Hachette Book Group, Inc.
1290 Avenue of the Americas
New York, NY 10104
workman.com

WORKMAN is a registered trademark of Workman Publishing Co., Inc., a subsidiary of Hachette Book Group, Inc.

Printed in China on responsibly sourced paper
First printing August 2017

10 9 8 7 6 5 4

CONTENTS

Welcome to the World of Miniature Aviation

IN MOST WAYS, mini paper airplanes are much like full-size paper planes. They fly for the same reasons and are adjusted in the same way, but little planes do have some special characteristics. They are more agile than their bigger counterparts—they turn faster and are more sensitive to adjustments. Their smaller size also gives them the appearance of being very fast (even though they actually fly at the same speed as bigger paper planes). Mini planes are ideal for indoor flying—in part because there's no wind to buffet them about or to carry them off, and also because they're so tiny, it's easy to lose them outdoors.

BEST-BET FOLDING TIPS

All the pocket flyers are marked with dashed and dotted lines. The dashed lines are what we call "fold-in" lines, which means that they will be on the inside of a crease; you won't be able to see them once you make the fold. They are numbered in the order you should make the folds.

The dotted lines are "fold-away" lines. You'll be able to see them on the outside of the crease; they act as guides to help you know that you're folding in the right place. Some planes require cutting; cut lines are indicated by thick solid lines.

Try to make your creases as sharp as possible. It's wise to run a fingernail over the edge after you make a fold. This will especially help with the planes that have a lot of folds in one area, like the Mini World Record.

ADJUSTING THE PLANES

Even if you've folded your plane exactly as indicated, there's a good chance that it won't fly well at first. Almost all paper airplanes need a little fine-tuning. Bear in mind that with small paper airplanes, even tiny adjustments can have extreme results. For example, if a little "up elevator" is required for a level glide, adding only a small amount more may cause the plane to loop.

DIHEDRAL

Most planes fly best if the wings form a slight "Y" shape with the body.

The first thing to check is that the wings are even and form a slight "Y" shape with the body. (In aviation speak, this is called dihedral.)

UP AND DOWN

Adjusting the elevator is probably the next most important fix—it can keep your plane from stalling (slowing, then swooping to the ground and crashing) or diving. The elevator on a paper airplane is usually located at the back edges of the wings. If your plane is diving, add a little up elevator by bending the back edges of the wings up a little. If it's stalling, you may have added too much up elevator. Flatten the back edges of the wings.

ELEVATOR

Adjust elevator up or down at the back edges of the wings.

LEFT AND RIGHT

Most paper airplanes have a tendency to turn when they are first thrown. This can be fixed by adjusting the rudder of the plane. On most paper airplanes, the rudder is the back of the body (fuselage). To adjust it, bend it a little to the right or left. If your plane isn't flying straight, bend the rudder in the direction you want it to go. For example, if your plane is veering off to the right, bend the rudder a little to the left, and vice versa. If your plane flies straight and you want it to turn right, bend the rudder to the right. Do the opposite for the left.

SENDING THEM SOARING

A good flight requires a good throw. For most planes, your best bet is to pinch the body (fuselage) toward the front, using your thumb and index finger. Hold the plane level just in front of your shoulder and toss it forward. The goal is to throw it straight, with the wings level.

LOOPS AND DIVES

The RKO, Mini World Record, and Cosmojet are all good planes for stunt flying.

To do loops, add a lot of up elevator to your plane—much more than you usually would. Hold your plane a little behind your shoulder and give it a gentle toss straight up. Your plane should climb a few feet, stop, flip over backward, dive at the ground, then pull up before hitting the floor.

You also need a lot of up elevator for dives. Hold your plane as high above your head as you can and a little in front of you. Point the nose straight down and drop the plane. It should swoop down and pull out of the dive before it hits the floor.

EXPERIMENT!

Each model in this book is unique. Experimentation is the quickest way to learn how a plane flies best. Test-fly your planes, trying different adjustments and faster and slower throws. Generally speaking, the larger and wider the wings, the slower an airplane can successfully fly and the better it will glide. Airplanes with smaller wings usually fly faster and are better suited for long distances. But don't accept our word on this; fold up some planes and find out for yourself!

RUDDER ——→

Bend the rudder in the direction you want your plane to go.

STAR QUEST

THE STAR QUEST has a Leading Edge Extension (LEX), a narrow portion of the wing extending forward to the nose. Current jet fighters such as the F/A-18 Hornet have a LEX to improve their maneuverability. Your plane is also maneuverable, and excels at swift, straight flights indoors or out.

FLYING TIPS | The Star Quest flies best if the wings form a slight "Y" shape with the body and it has plenty of up elevator.

Making the Star Quest

Cut on solid lines; fold in on dashed lines (so they are no longer visible); fold away on dotted lines.

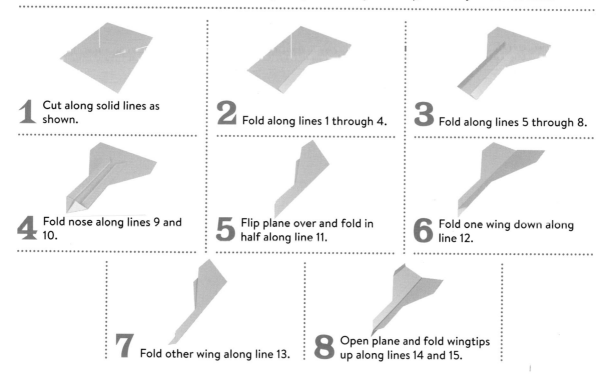

1 Cut along solid lines as shown.

2 Fold along lines 1 through 4.

3 Fold along lines 5 through 8.

4 Fold nose along lines 9 and 10.

5 Flip plane over and fold in half along line 11.

6 Fold one wing down along line 12.

7 Fold other wing along line 13.

8 Open plane and fold wingtips up along lines 14 and 15.

AEROBOT

IT'S A SPACECRAFT! It's a robot! It's both! The Aerobot was inspired by joined-wing planes—which can be thought of as biplanes with wings joined at the tips—a concept NASA has studied. Sometimes the Aerobot develops a mind of its own and rolls and turns as it flies.

FLYING TIPS

You can control how straight the Aerobot flies by adding a paper clip to the nose. No paper clip results in erratic flight; adding one yields a smoother flight.

Making the Aerobot

Fold in on dashed lines (so they are no longer visible); fold away on dotted lines.

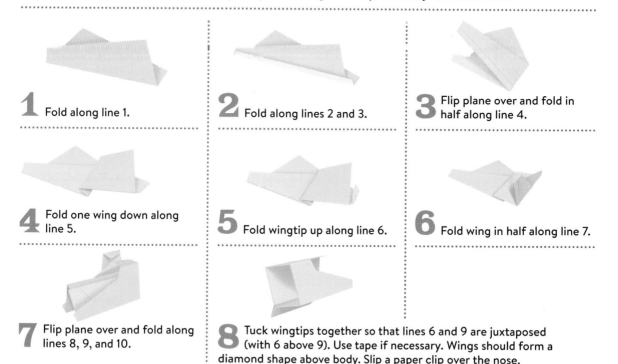

1 Fold along line 1.

2 Fold along lines 2 and 3.

3 Flip plane over and fold in half along line 4.

4 Fold one wing down along line 5.

5 Fold wingtip up along line 6.

6 Fold wing in half along line 7.

7 Flip plane over and fold along lines 8, 9, and 10.

8 Tuck wingtips together so that lines 6 and 9 are juxtaposed (with 6 above 9). Use tape if necessary. Wings should form a diamond shape above body. Slip a paper clip over the nose.

ARDOR

HERE'S A PLANE that's designed to stir emotions fitting to its name. It's an excellent all-around flyer—fast and true. Use it to send a message straight from the heart to someone you care about (really!—use a Sharpie to write on the plane and let it fly).

FLYING TIPS | This plane flies best with a little up elevator. Use more up elevator and some rudder for turns: right rudder for right turns, left for left. Make sure wings form a slight "Y" shape with the body.

Making the Ardor

Cut on solid lines; fold in on dashed lines (so they are no longer visible); fold away on dotted lines.

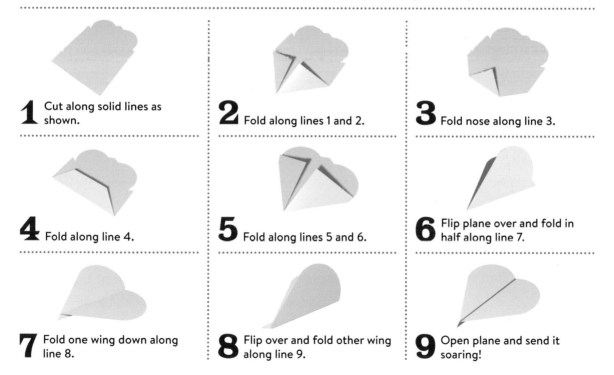

1 Cut along solid lines as shown.

2 Fold along lines 1 and 2.

3 Fold nose along line 3.

4 Fold along line 4.

5 Fold along lines 5 and 6.

6 Flip plane over and fold in half along line 7.

7 Fold one wing down along line 8.

8 Flip over and fold other wing along line 9.

9 Open plane and send it soaring!

ALIEN CLIPPER

BE PREPARED FOR a close encounter of the third kind! This plane is best suited for fast, straight flights, either down the hall or across the yard. It's a great distance flier— see how many feet yours will go.

FLYING TIPS

The Alien Clipper flies best if the wings form a slight "Y" shape with the body, and with some up elevator. Experiment with flying it with the wingtips pointed straight up, or straight down, but beware of the "death spiral" that can result if the wingtips are straight out (level with the wing).

Making the Alien Clipper

Cut on solid lines; fold in on dashed lines (so they are no longer visible); fold away on dotted lines.

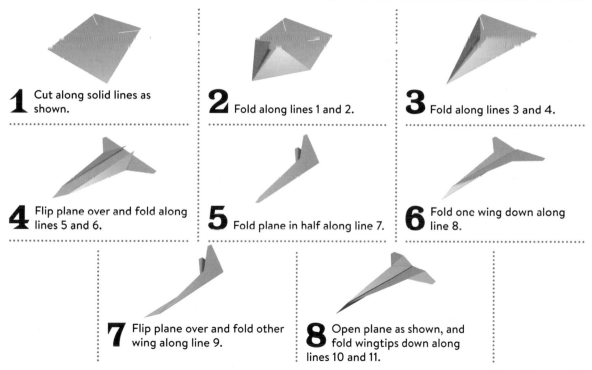

1 Cut along solid lines as shown.

2 Fold along lines 1 and 2.

3 Fold along lines 3 and 4.

4 Flip plane over and fold along lines 5 and 6.

5 Fold plane in half along line 7.

6 Fold one wing down along line 8.

7 Flip plane over and fold other wing along line 9.

8 Open plane as shown, and fold wingtips down along lines 10 and 11.

RKO

THIS PLANE WAS built to rock and roll. It's a versatile flyer, excelling at both zipping across the room and floating in circles. With practice, you can even get it to perform loops. Pick it up and tune in to some great flying today!

FLYING TIPS | This plane flies best with a little up elevator. Use more up elevator for loops and dives. Make sure the wings form a slight "Y" shape with the body.

Making the RKO

Fold in on dashed lines (so they are no longer visible); fold away on dotted lines.

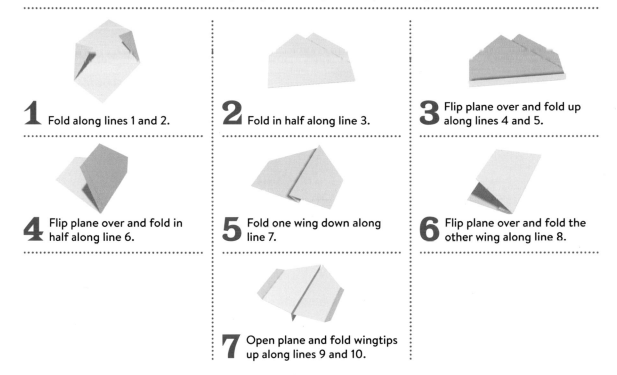

1 Fold along lines 1 and 2.

2 Fold in half along line 3.

3 Flip plane over and fold up along lines 4 and 5.

4 Flip plane over and fold in half along line 6.

5 Fold one wing down along line 7.

6 Flip plane over and fold the other wing along line 8.

7 Open plane and fold wingtips up along lines 9 and 10.

SPECTRE

THE SPECTRE FEATURES an advanced wing design that's been used for supersonic flight. The combination of two different sweep angles on the wing's leading edge makes it more efficient at both high speed for cruising and low speed for taking off and landing. This paper model may not be high-tech, but it's a swift and steady flyer.

FLYING TIPS | This airplane needs plenty of up elevator to keep it from diving. Make sure wings form a slight "Y" shape with body. If you like, tape down folds on leading edge.

Making the Spectre

Cut on solid lines; fold in on dashed lines (so they are no longer visible); fold away on dotted lines.

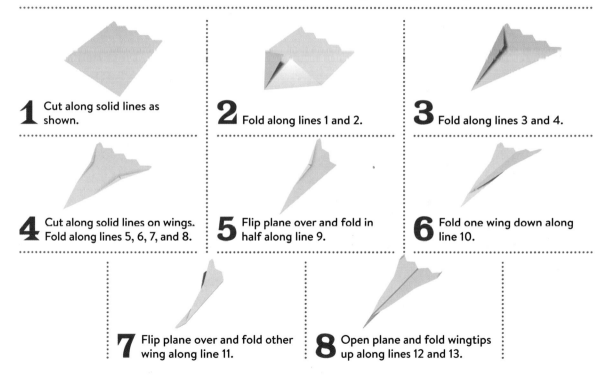

1 Cut along solid lines as shown.

2 Fold along lines 1 and 2.

3 Fold along lines 3 and 4.

4 Cut along solid lines on wings. Fold along lines 5, 6, 7, and 8.

5 Flip plane over and fold in half along line 9.

6 Fold one wing down along line 10.

7 Flip plane over and fold other wing along line 11.

8 Open plane and fold wingtips up along lines 12 and 13.

GEMINI

THESE TWIN ROCKETS are bound at the hip, forever following the same trajectory. Like their real-life forebears at NASA, they are a great choice for distance and accuracy. See if you can get them to land on the "moon" across the room.

FLYING TIPS

This plane needs a little up elevator for best flying. The points at the front of the plane can get bent after flying; before each flight, make sure they are straight.

Making the Gemini

Cut on solid line; fold in on dashed lines (so they are no longer visible); fold away on dotted lines.

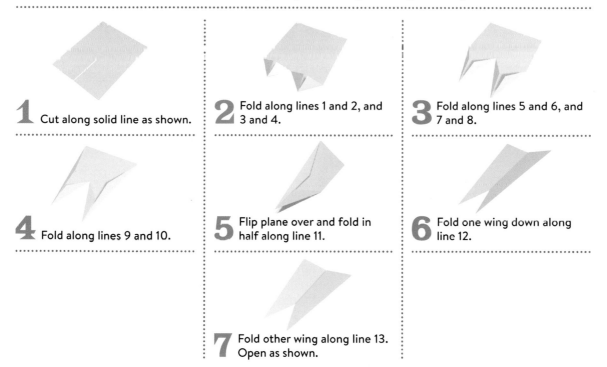

1 Cut along solid line as shown.

2 Fold along lines 1 and 2, and 3 and 4.

3 Fold along lines 5 and 6, and 7 and 8.

4 Fold along lines 9 and 10.

5 Flip plane over and fold in half along line 11.

6 Fold one wing down along line 12.

7 Fold other wing along line 13. Open as shown.

MINI WORLD RECORD PAPER AIRPLANE

THIS MAY NOT look like a spectacular plane, but it is. It's great for general flying, aerobatics, and—in its larger form—setting world records! Ken Blackburn used the full-size version of this model to set the Guinness world record for time aloft four times.

FLYING TIPS | For general flying, bend the elevator up a little; for loops and dives, bend it up a lot. Time aloft (world record) flights require a hard throw straight up and a high ceiling.

Making the Mini World Record

Fold in on dashed lines (so they are no longer visible); fold away on dotted lines.

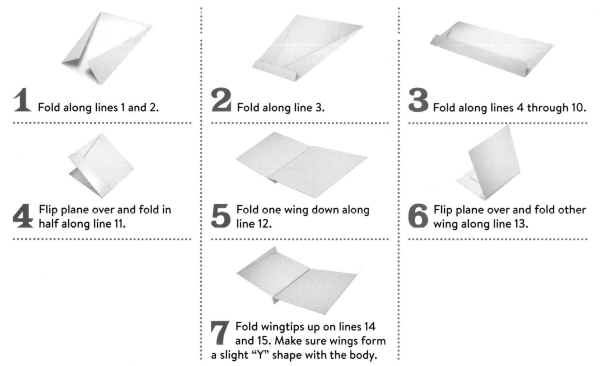

1 Fold along lines 1 and 2.

2 Fold along line 3.

3 Fold along lines 4 through 10.

4 Flip plane over and fold in half along line 11.

5 Fold one wing down along line 12.

6 Flip plane over and fold other wing along line 13.

7 Fold wingtips up on lines 14 and 15. Make sure wings form a slight "Y" shape with the body.

SPACE STATION

THIS SPACE STATION may be smaller than the International Space Station, but it does allow you to perform suborbital research in your own backyard. It excels at straight, accurate flights.

FLYING TIPS | Add a little up elevator for best flying. For slow flights, bend the entire back edge of the wing up.

Making the Space Station

Cut on solid line; fold in on dashed lines (so they are no longer visible); fold away on dotted lines.

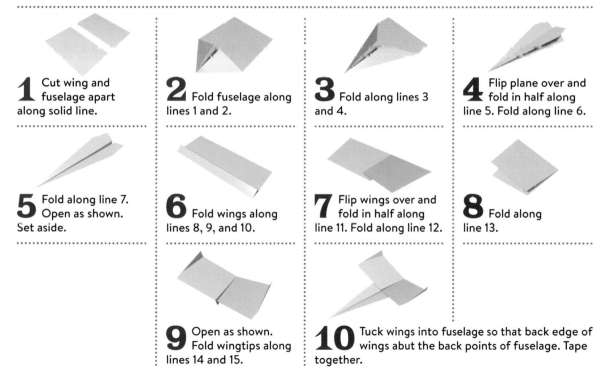

1 Cut wing and fuselage apart along solid line.

2 Fold fuselage along lines 1 and 2.

3 Fold along lines 3 and 4.

4 Flip plane over and fold in half along line 5. Fold along line 6.

5 Fold along line 7. Open as shown. Set aside.

6 Fold wings along lines 8, 9, and 10.

7 Flip wings over and fold in half along line 11. Fold along line 12.

8 Fold along line 13.

9 Open as shown. Fold wingtips along lines 14 and 15.

10 Tuck wings into fuselage so that back edge of wings abut the back points of fuselage. Tape together.

DYNAMO

GET READY TO fold up a shockingly good plane. Benjamin Franklin may have been the first person to combine flight and electricity when he used a kite to discover that lightning is actually a giant electric spark. You'll be following in his footsteps when you throw this 10,000-volt thunderbolt. The Dynamo is ideal for speedy, accurate flights.

FLYING TIPS | Use just a little up elevator for fast flights. Use more up elevator for longer, slower flying.

Making the Dynamo

Cut on solid lines; fold in on dashed lines (so they are no longer visible); fold away on dotted lines.

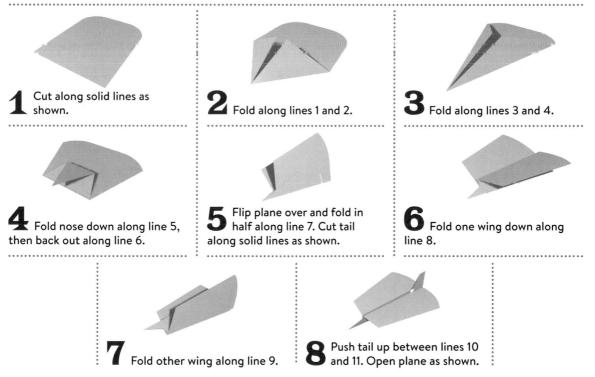

1 Cut along solid lines as shown.

2 Fold along lines 1 and 2.

3 Fold along lines 3 and 4.

4 Fold nose down along line 5, then back out along line 6.

5 Flip plane over and fold in half along line 7. Cut tail along solid lines as shown.

6 Fold one wing down along line 8.

7 Fold other wing along line 9.

8 Push tail up between lines 10 and 11. Open plane as shown.

GALAXY 800

THE GALAXY 800'S design is a 21st-century modification of the basic dart paper airplane. The points at the wingtips help add stability, which makes the plane ideally suited for long intergalactic flights and precision landings indoors and out.

FLYING TIPS

Some up elevator is required for smooth flights. Be sure the wings are either level or slightly angled upward so they form a "Y" shape when the plane is viewed from the front. The points on each wing should be level with the rest of the wing.

Making the Galaxy 800

Cut on solid lines; fold in on dashed lines (so they are no longer visible); fold away on dotted lines.

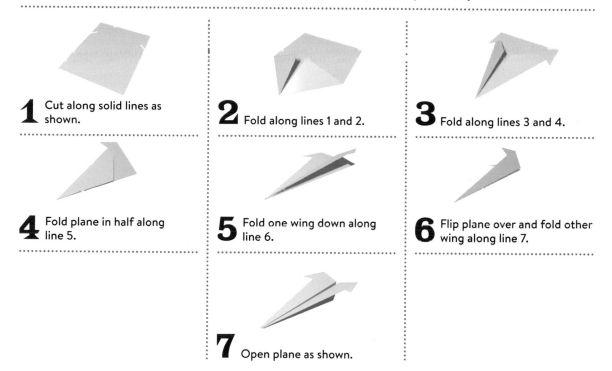

1 Cut along solid lines as shown.

2 Fold along lines 1 and 2.

3 Fold along lines 3 and 4.

4 Fold plane in half along line 5.

5 Fold one wing down along line 6.

6 Flip plane over and fold other wing along line 7.

7 Open plane as shown.

COSMOJET

WHO'S GOING TO defend the world from ill-tempered mutant robots? You will! The Cosmojet is well armed and can outmaneuver any evil force in your house. It is a solid flyer, well suited for precise flights across the room, or you can let it soar outside. It's also capable of doing loops and dives.

FLYING TIPS | The Cosmojet requires some up elevator for stable flights. If it dives, try bending the back half of the plane upward.

Making the Cosmojet

Cut on solid lines; fold in on dashed lines (so they are no longer visible); fold away on dotted lines.

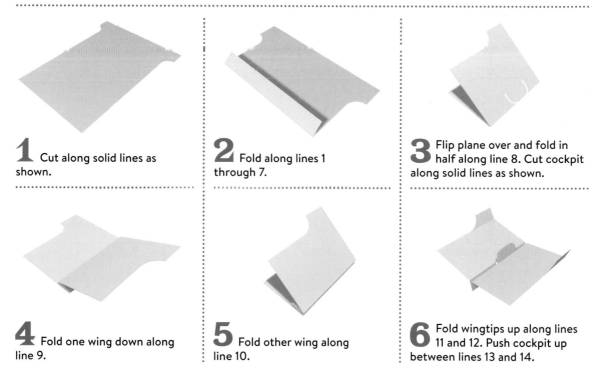

1 Cut along solid lines as shown.

2 Fold along lines 1 through 7.

3 Flip plane over and fold in half along line 8. Cut cockpit along solid lines as shown.

4 Fold one wing down along line 9.

5 Fold other wing along line 10.

6 Fold wingtips up along lines 11 and 12. Push cockpit up between lines 13 and 14.

Flight Log

Date	Airplane Name	Longest Time Aloft	Greatest Distance Flown

The Space Flyers Squadron

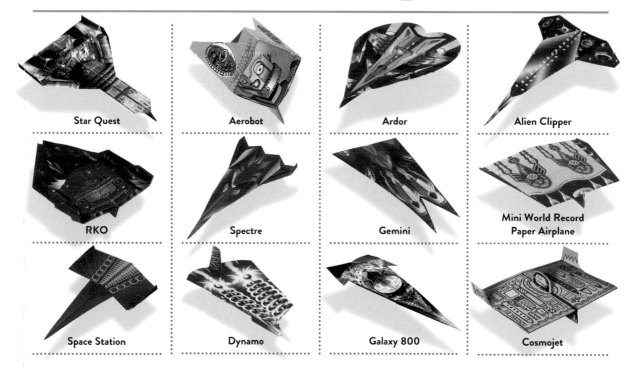

Star Quest

Aerobot

Ardor

Alien Clipper

RKO

Spectre

Gemini

Mini World Record
Paper Airplane

Space Station

Dynamo

Galaxy 800

Cosmojet

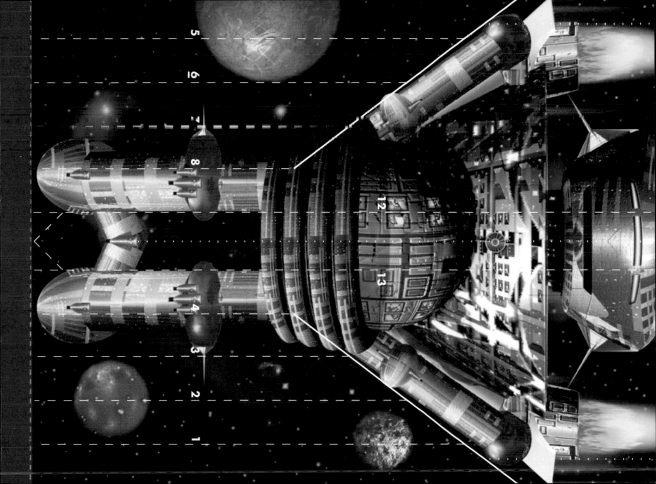

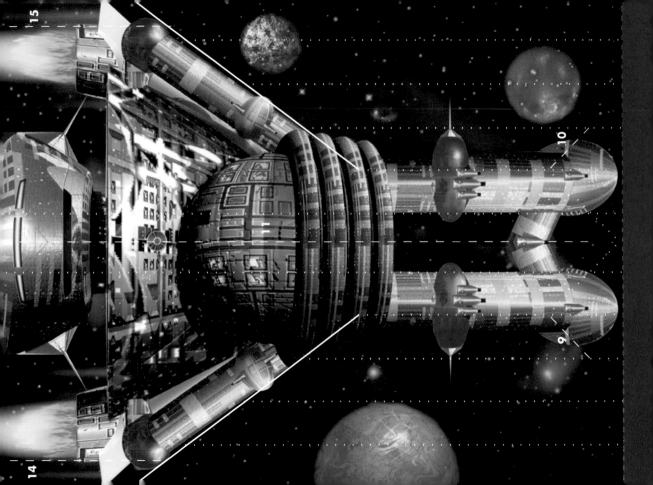

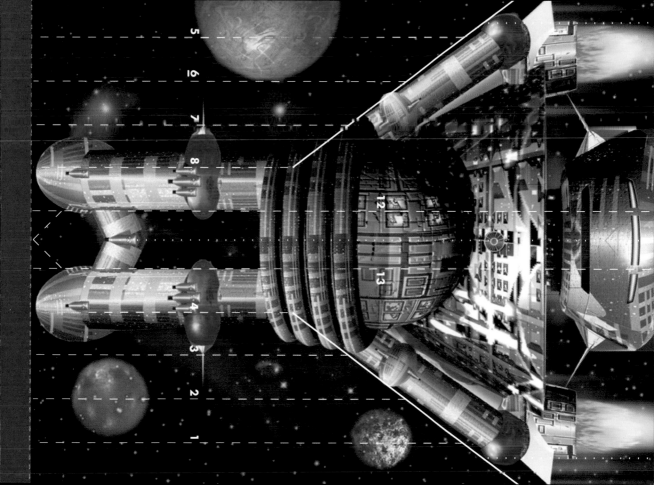

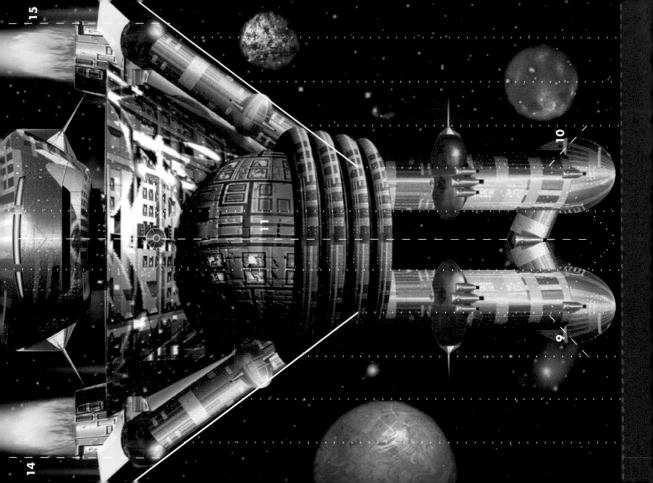

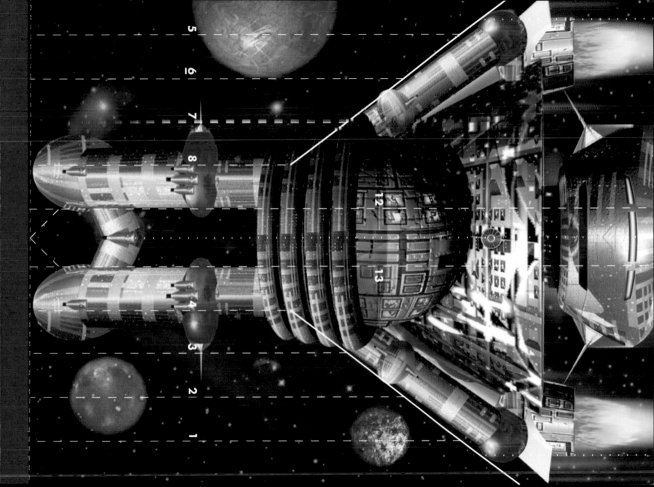

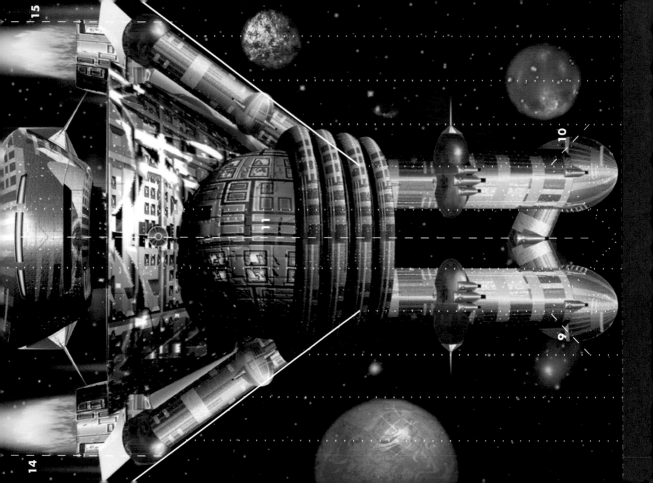

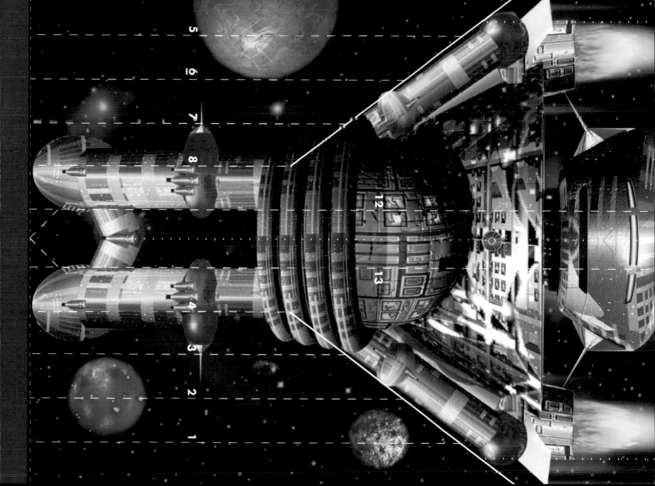

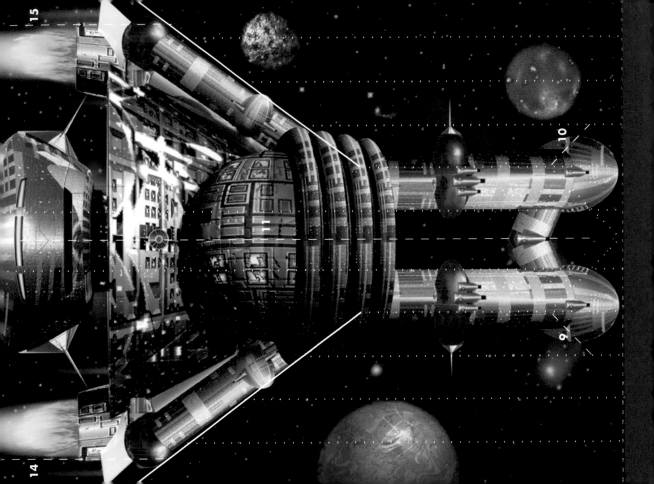

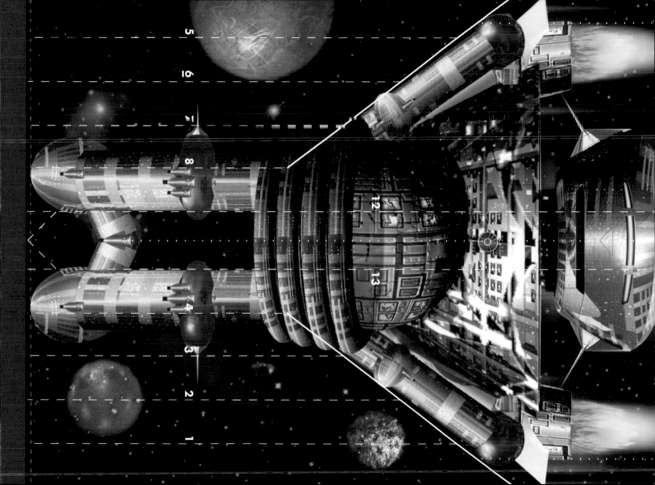

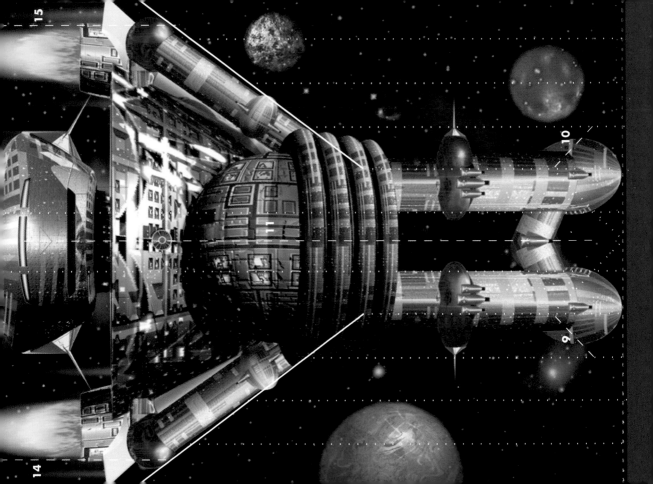

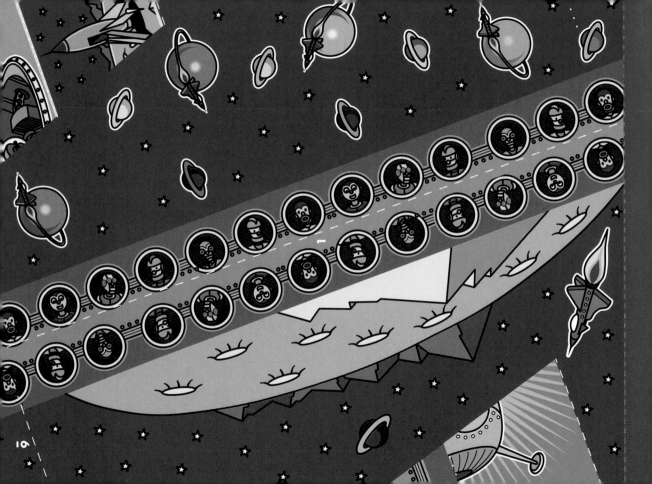

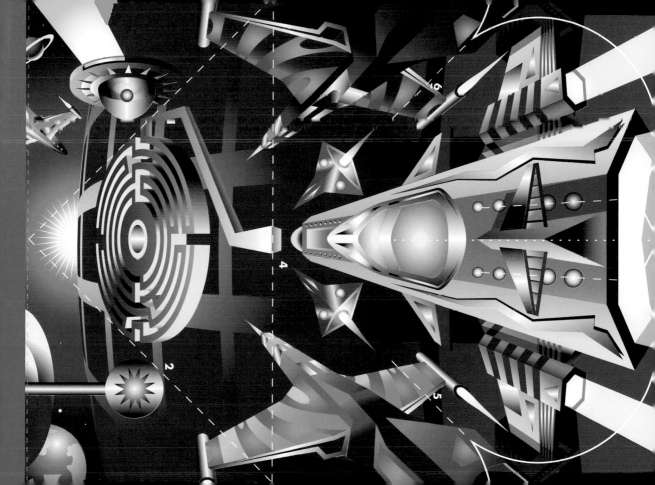

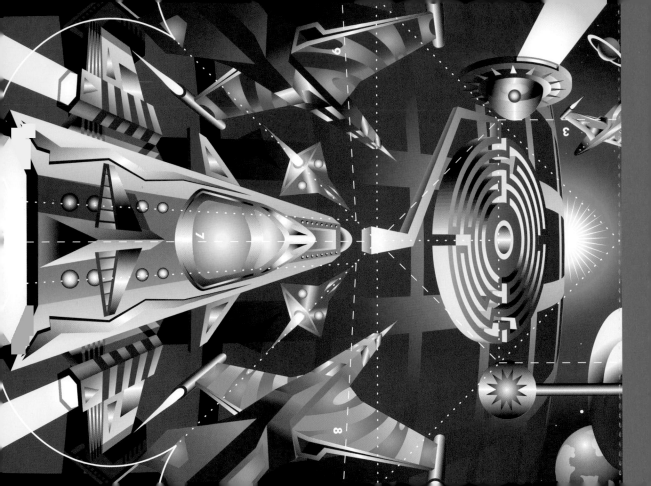

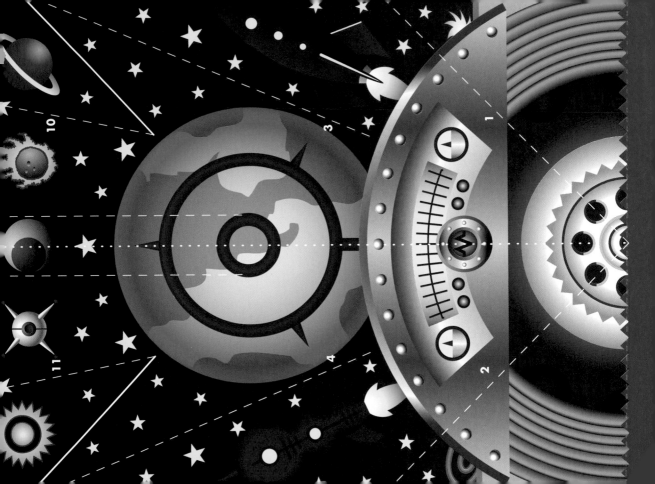

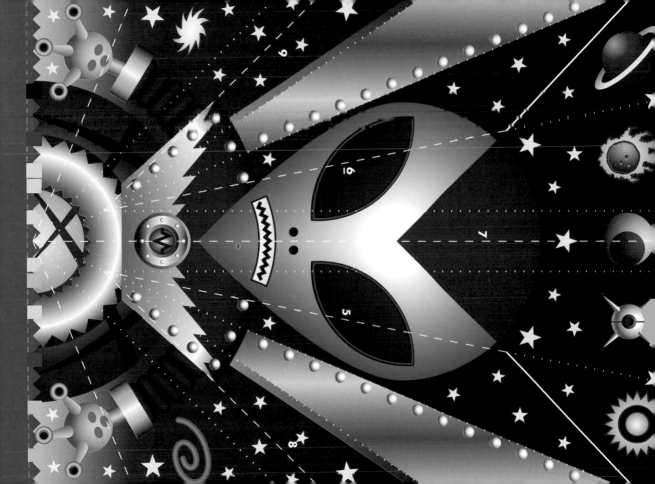

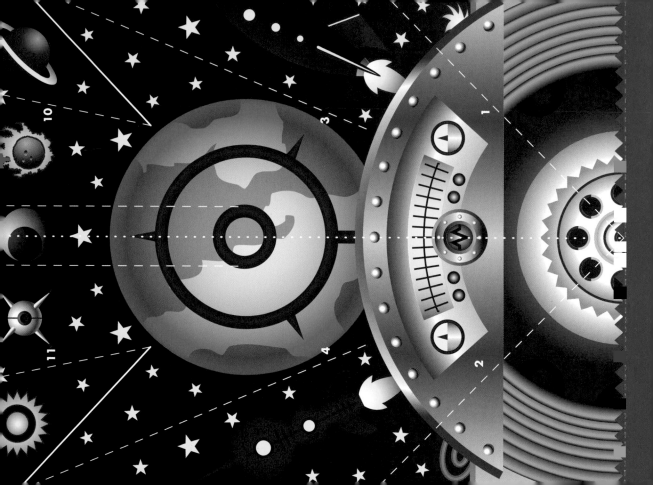

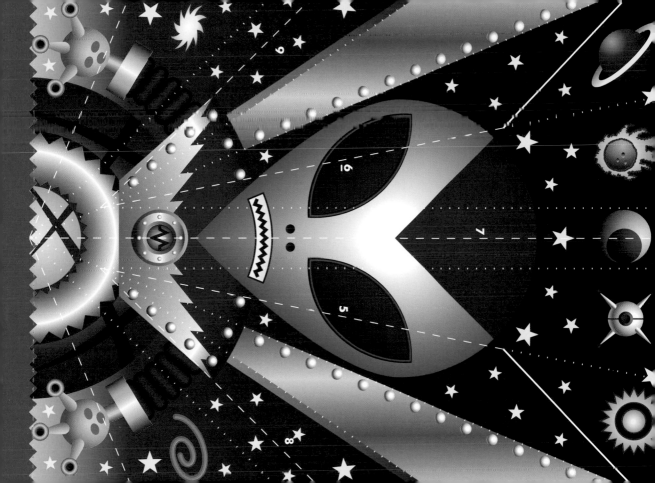

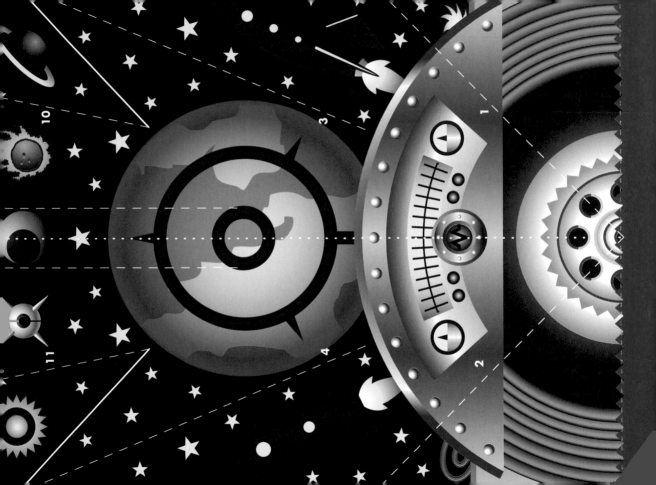

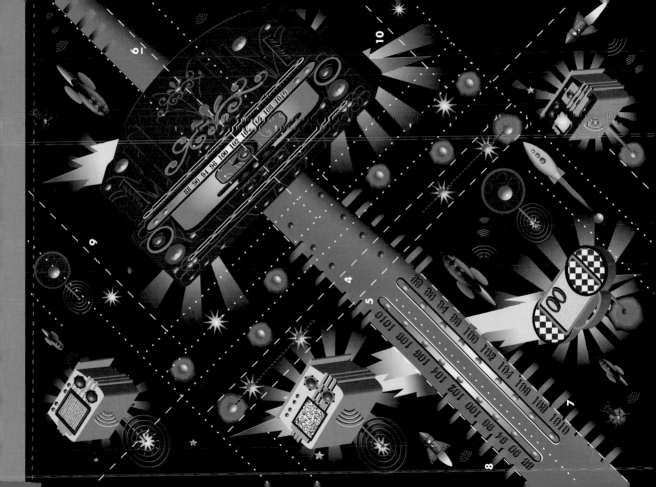

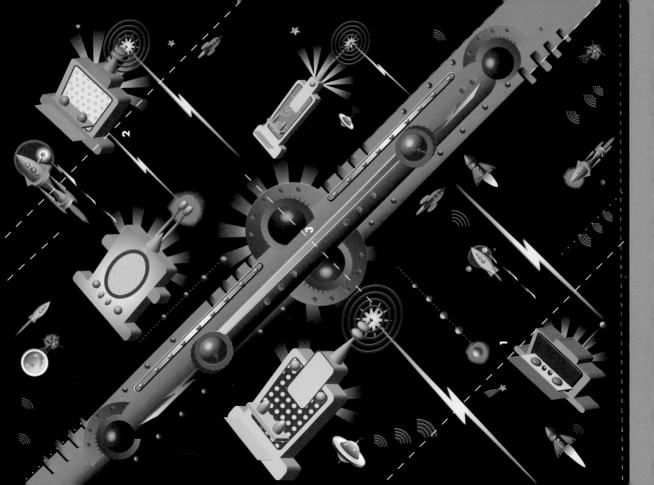

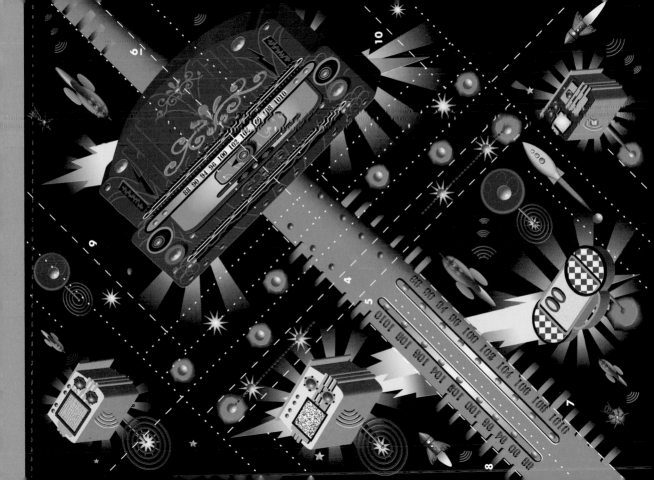

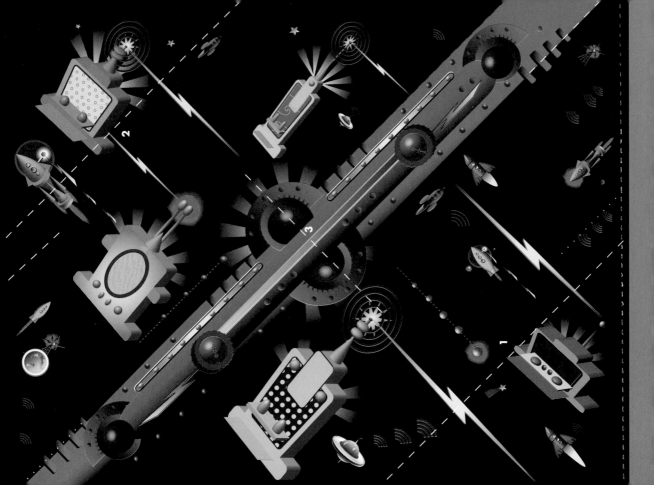

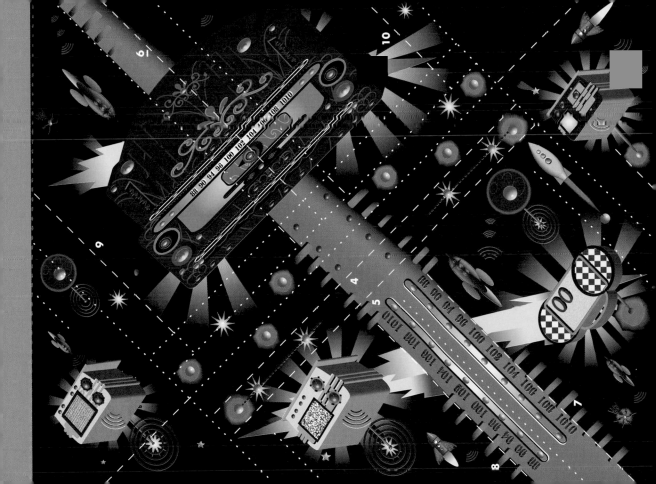

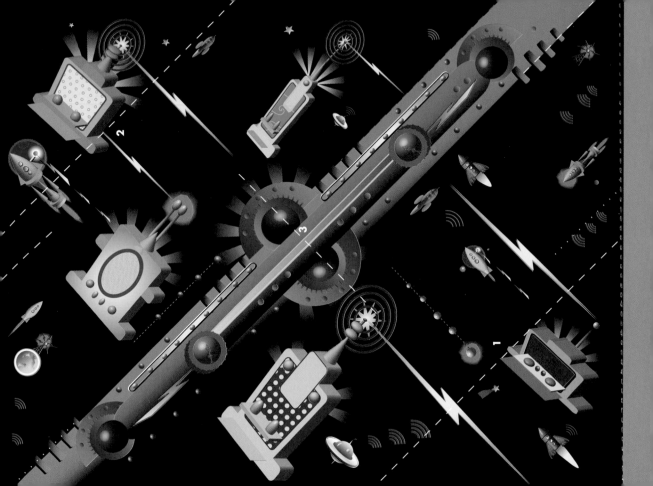

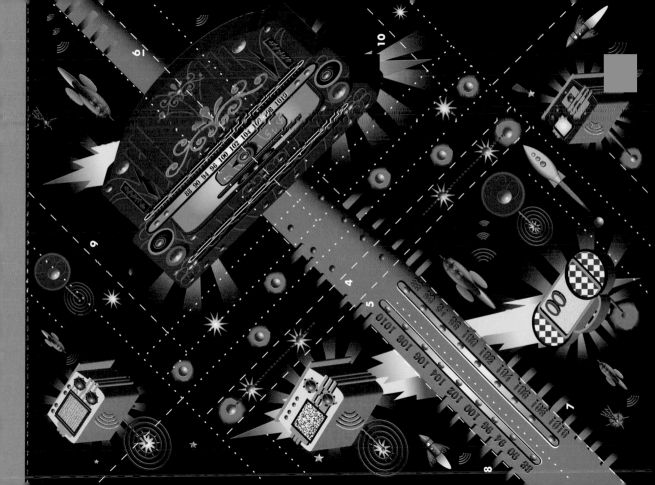

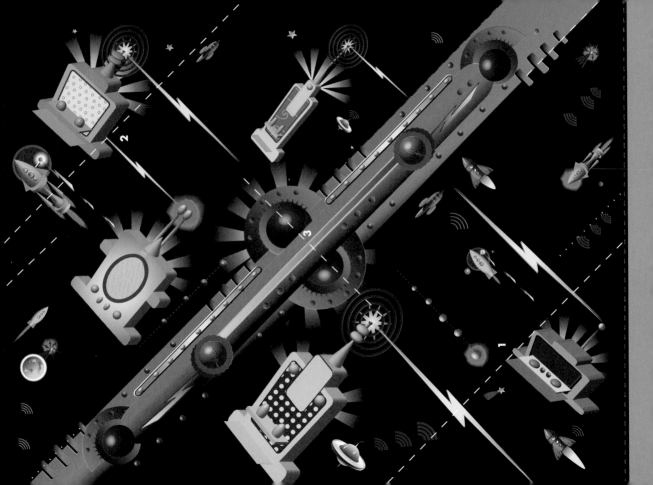

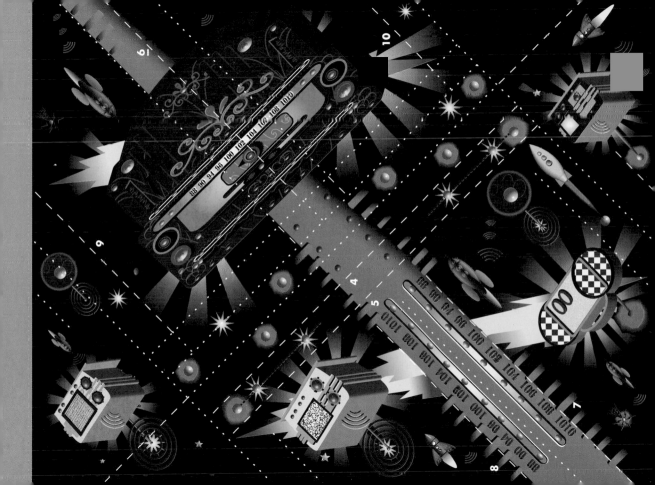

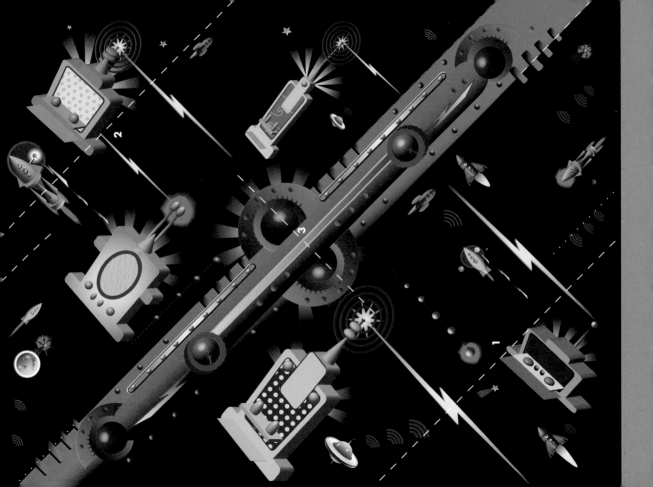

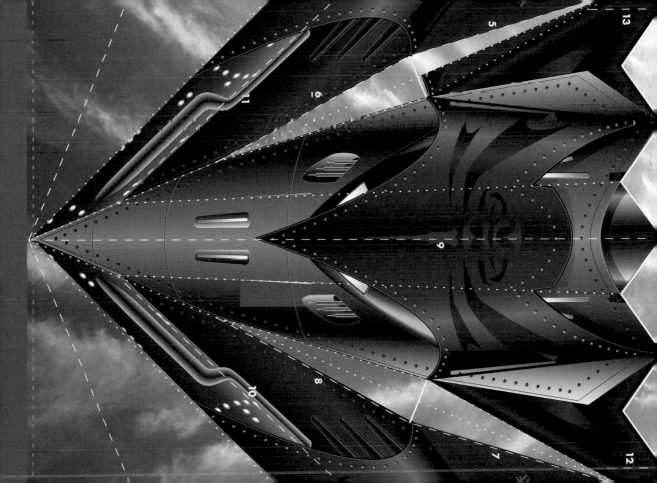

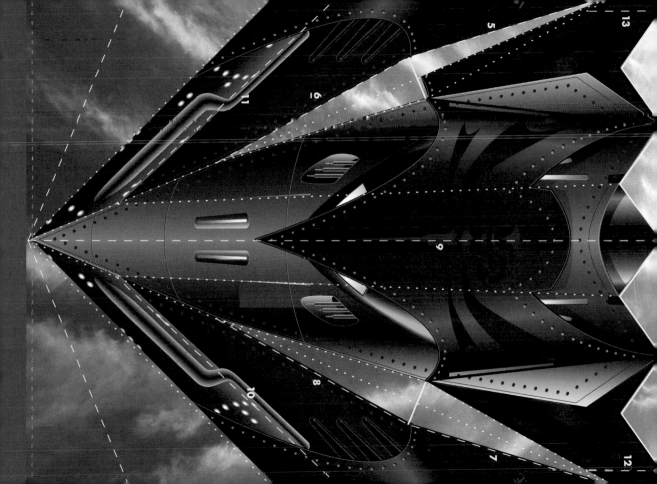

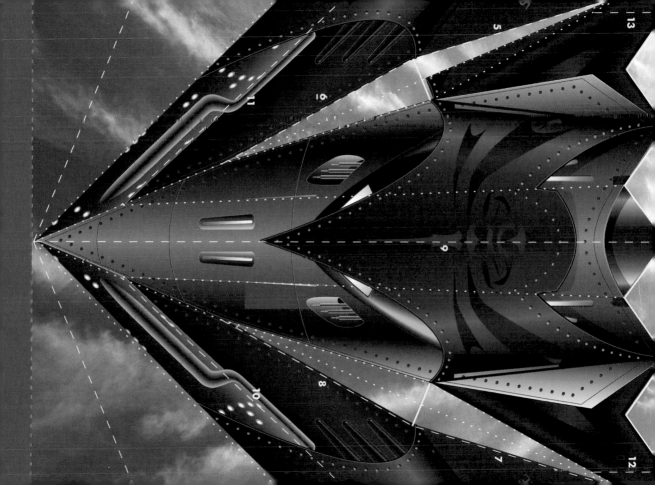

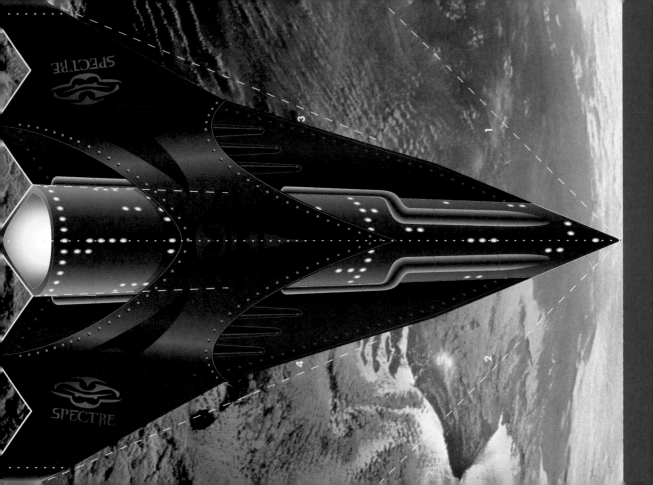

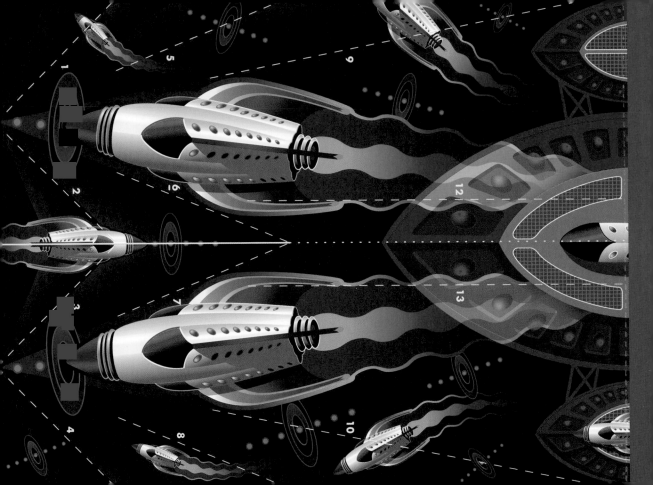

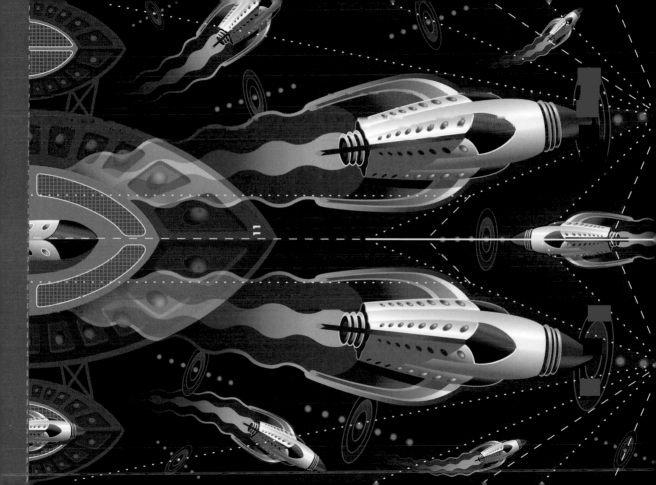

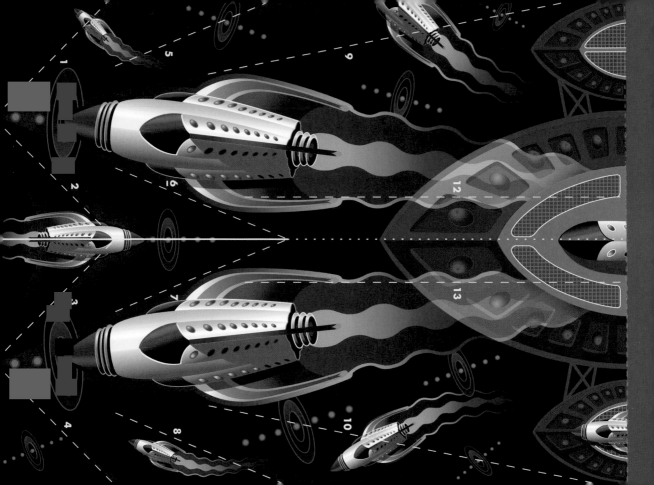

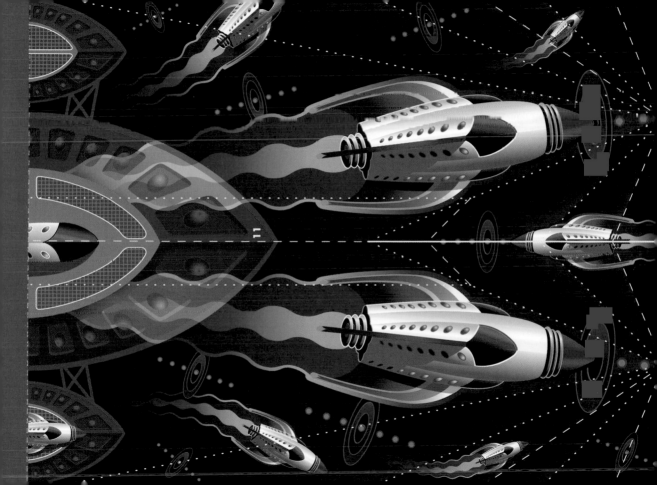

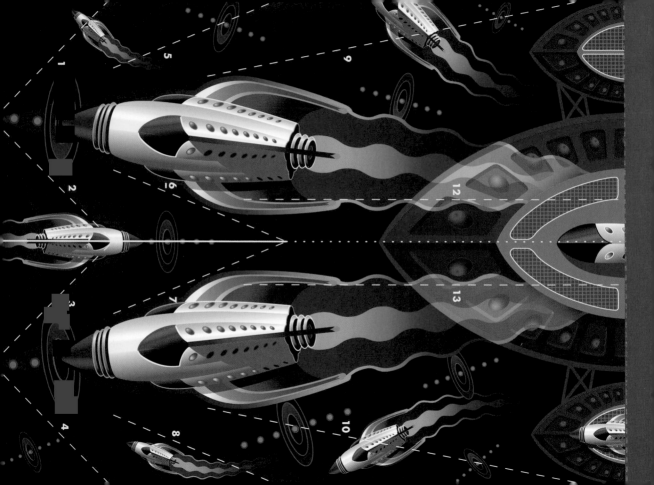

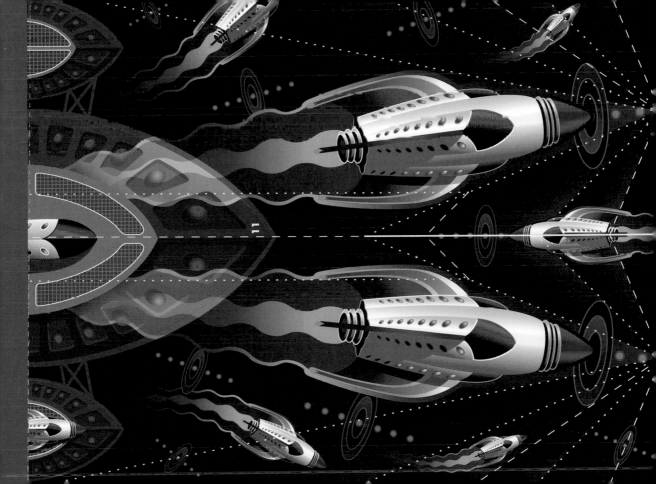

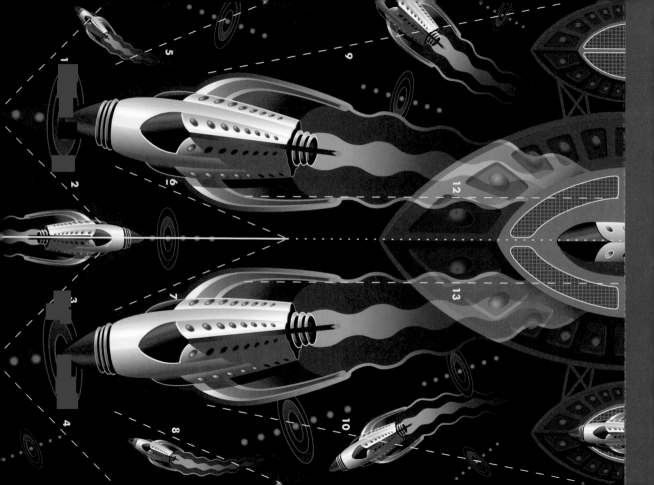

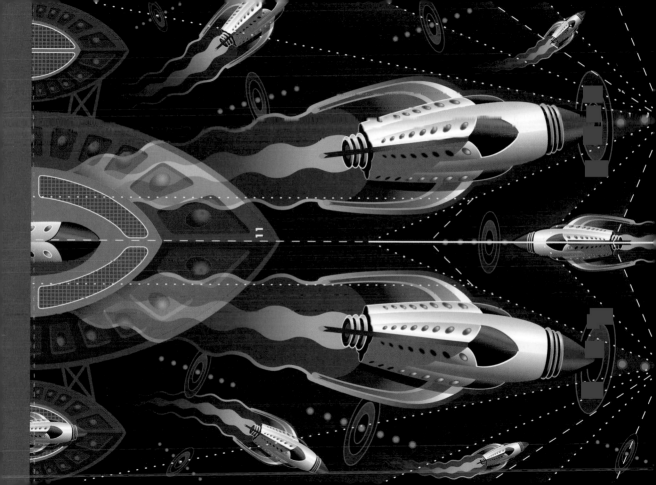

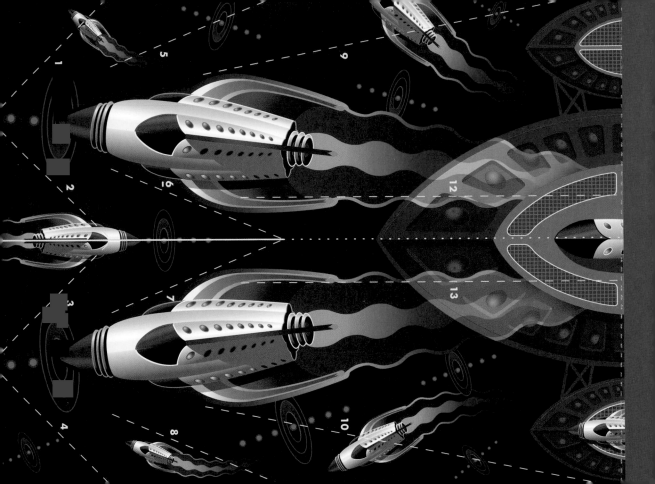

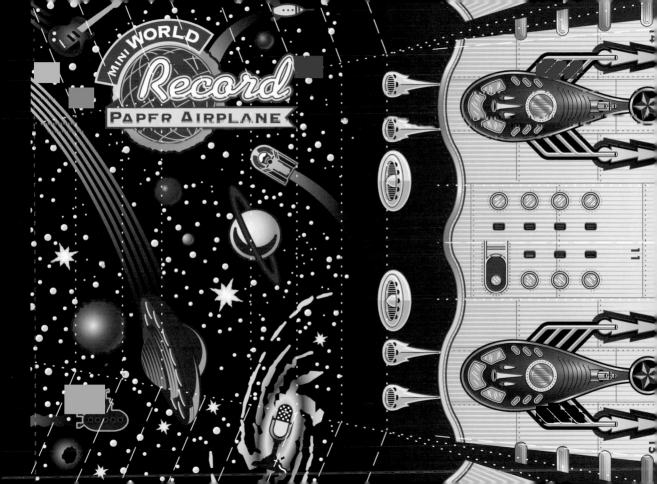

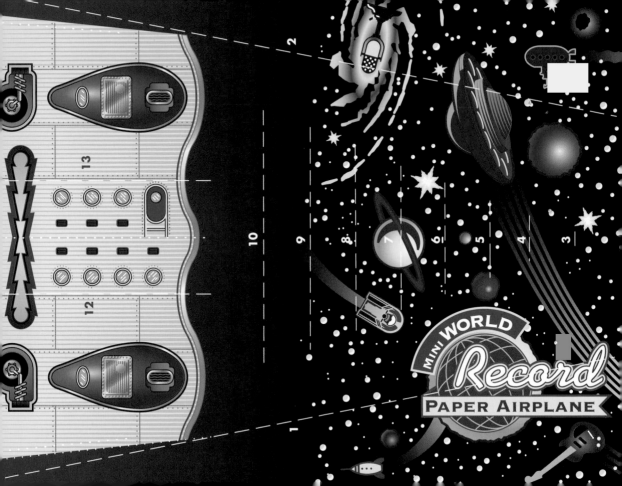

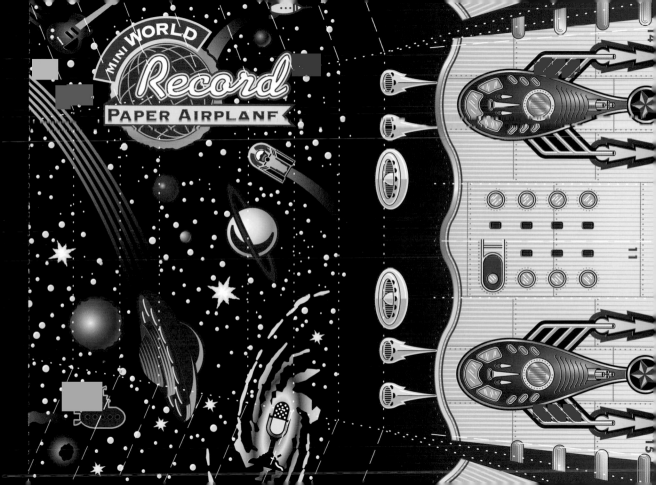

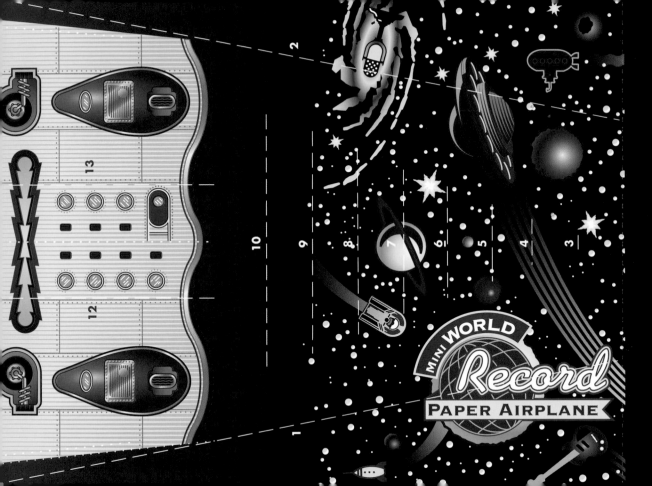

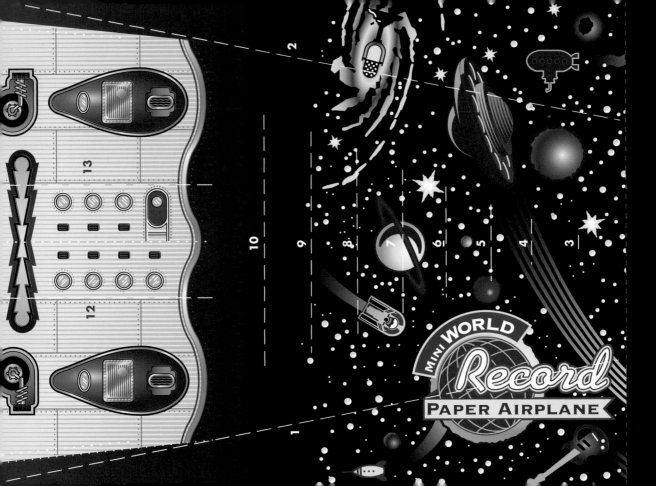

MINI WORLD
Record
PAPER AIRPLANE

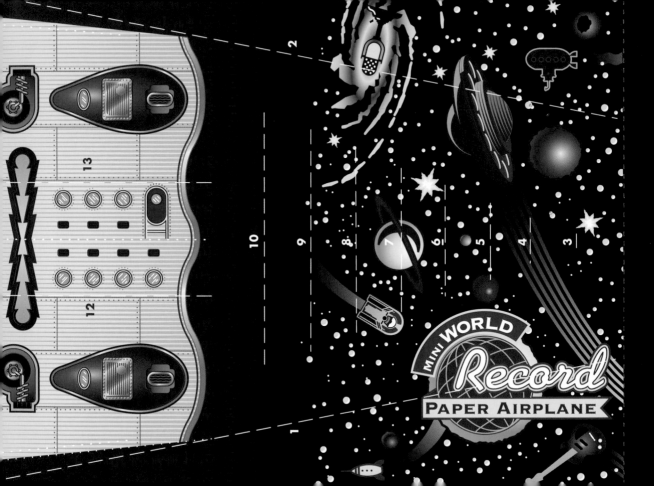

MINI WORLD
Record
PAPER AIRPLANE

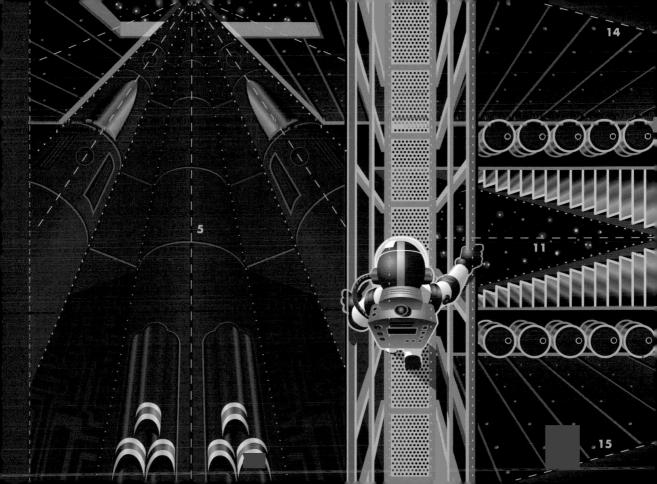

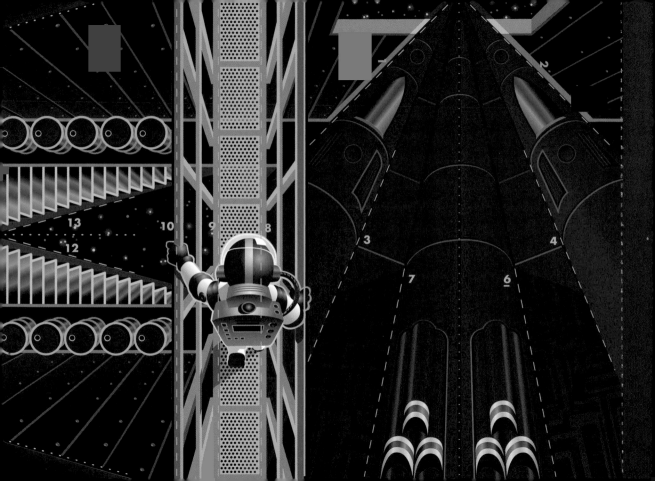

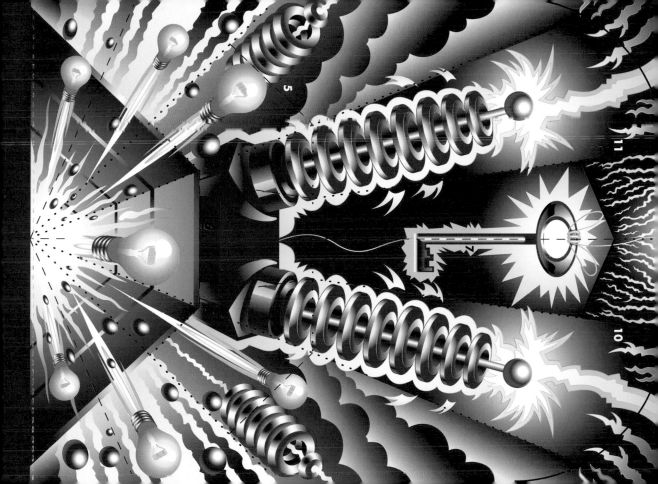

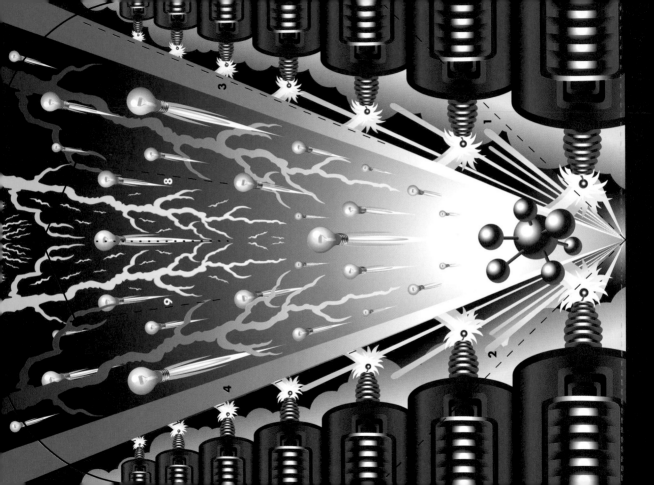

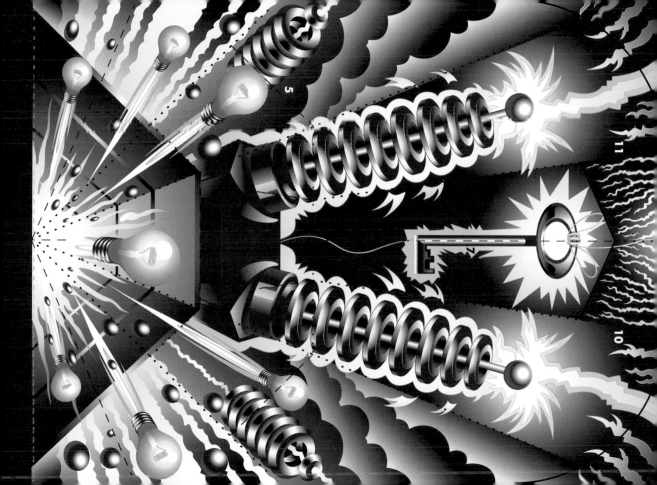

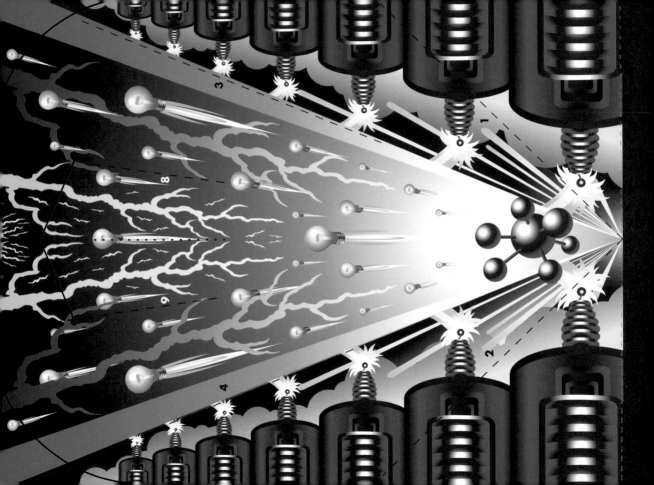

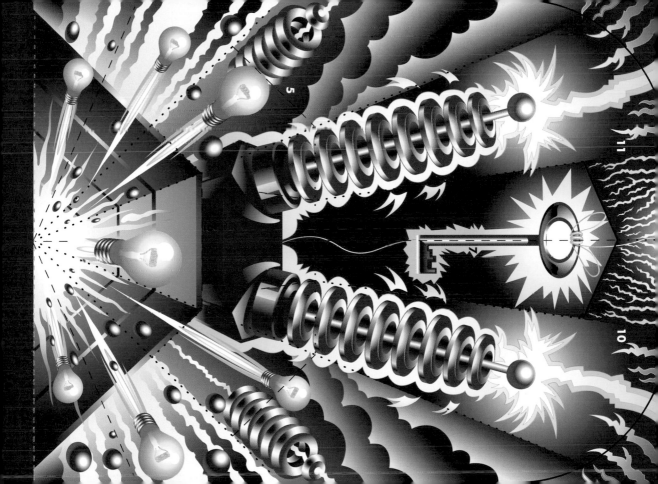

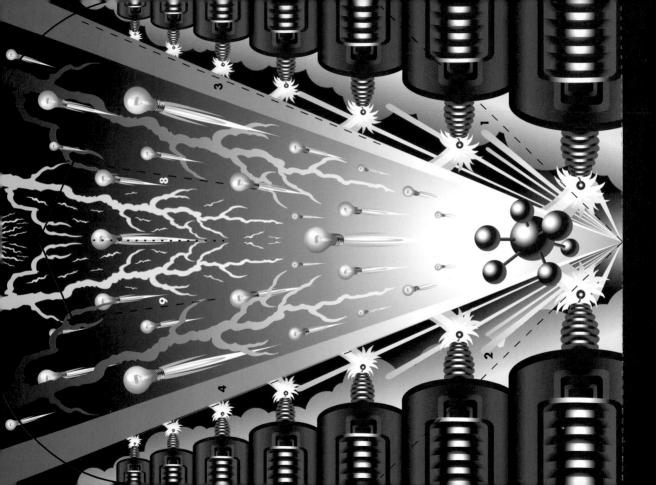

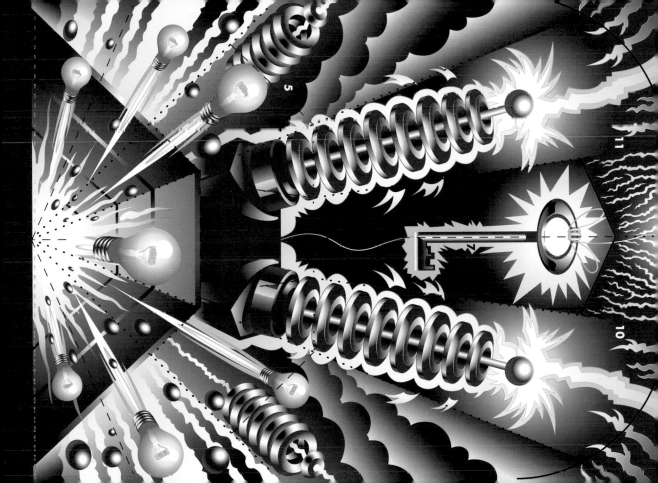

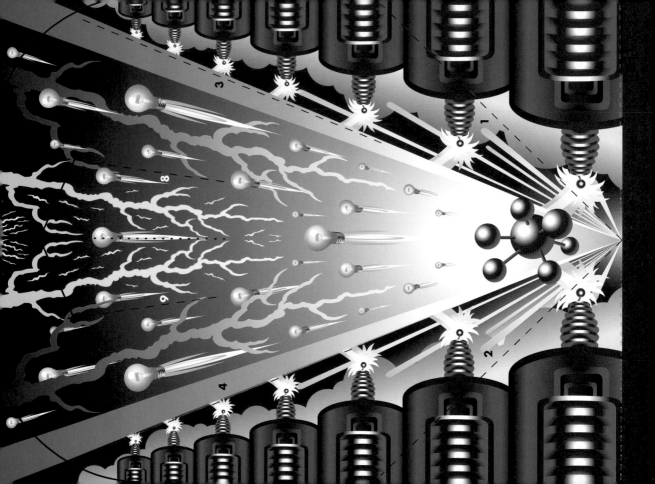

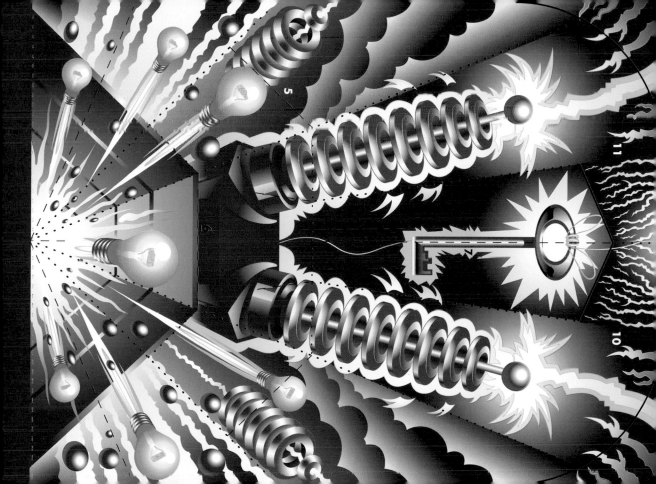

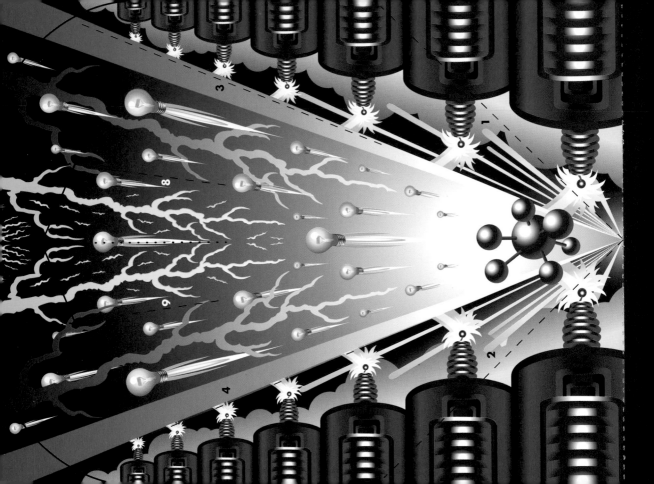

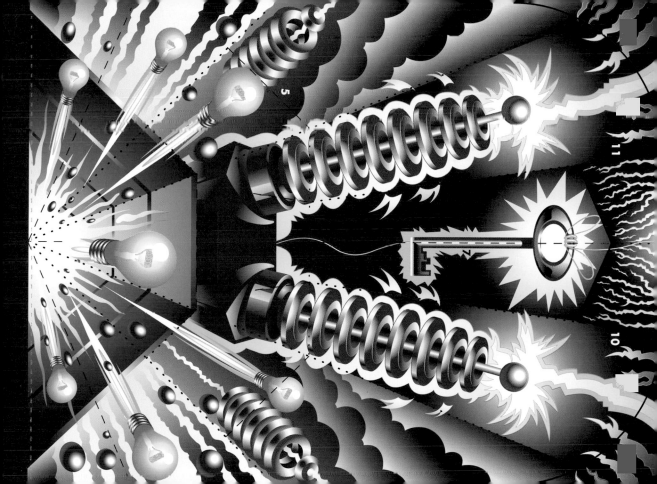

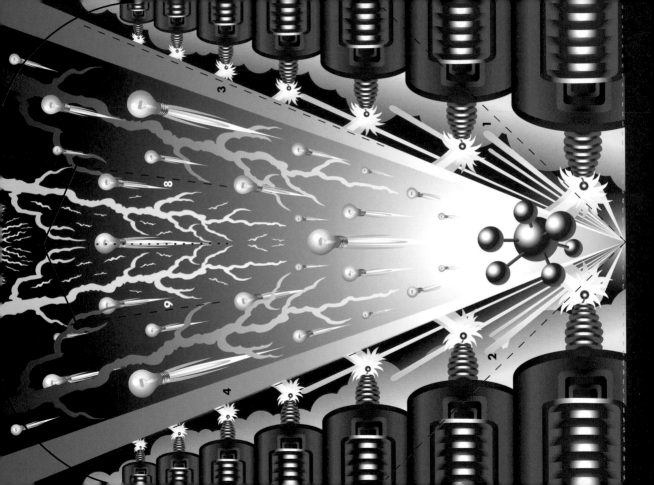

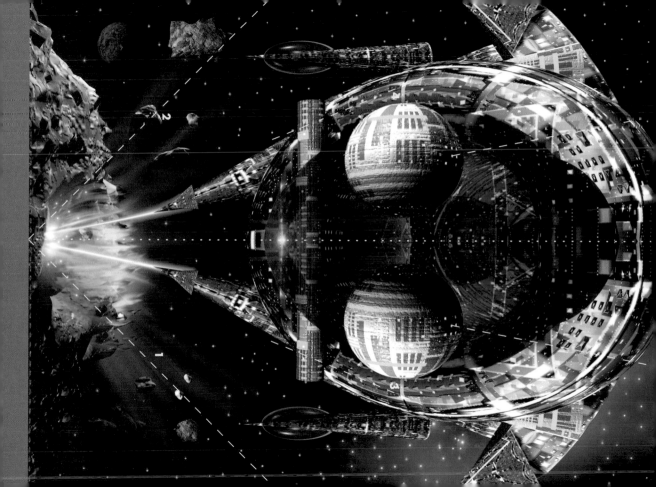

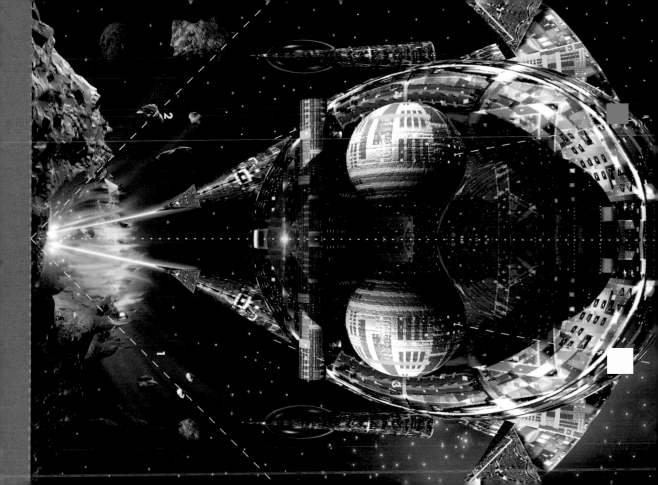

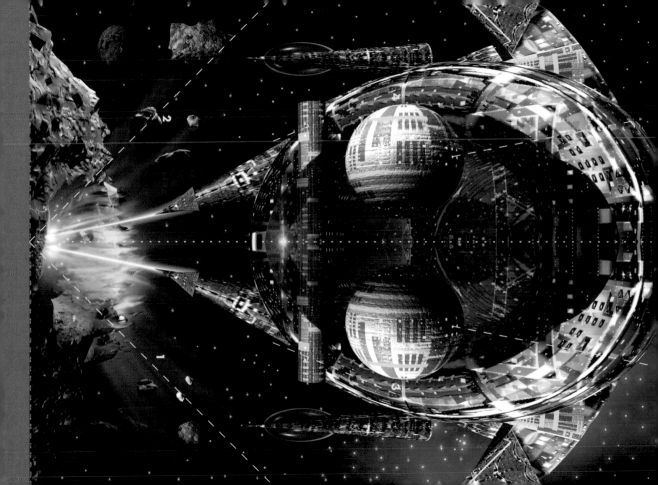

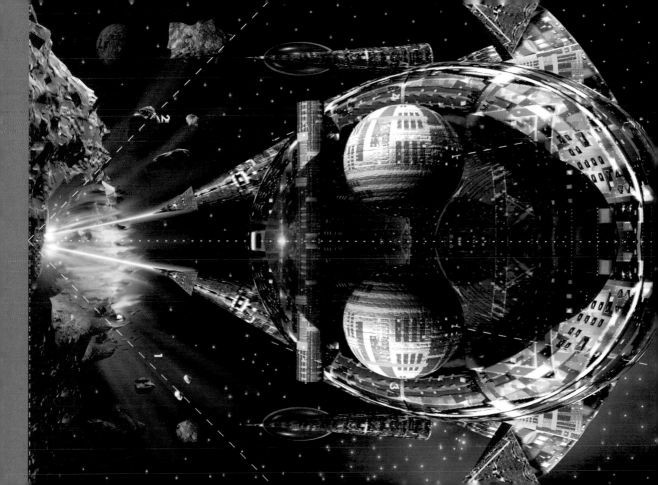